Just Cocks Coloring Book For Adults

Funny and Naughty Penis Coloring Book containing 25 Cock Coloring Pages filled with Paisley, Henna and Mandala Patterns.

by The Coloring Book People

ISBN-13: 978-1546480082

ISBN-10: 1546480080

Preview Page

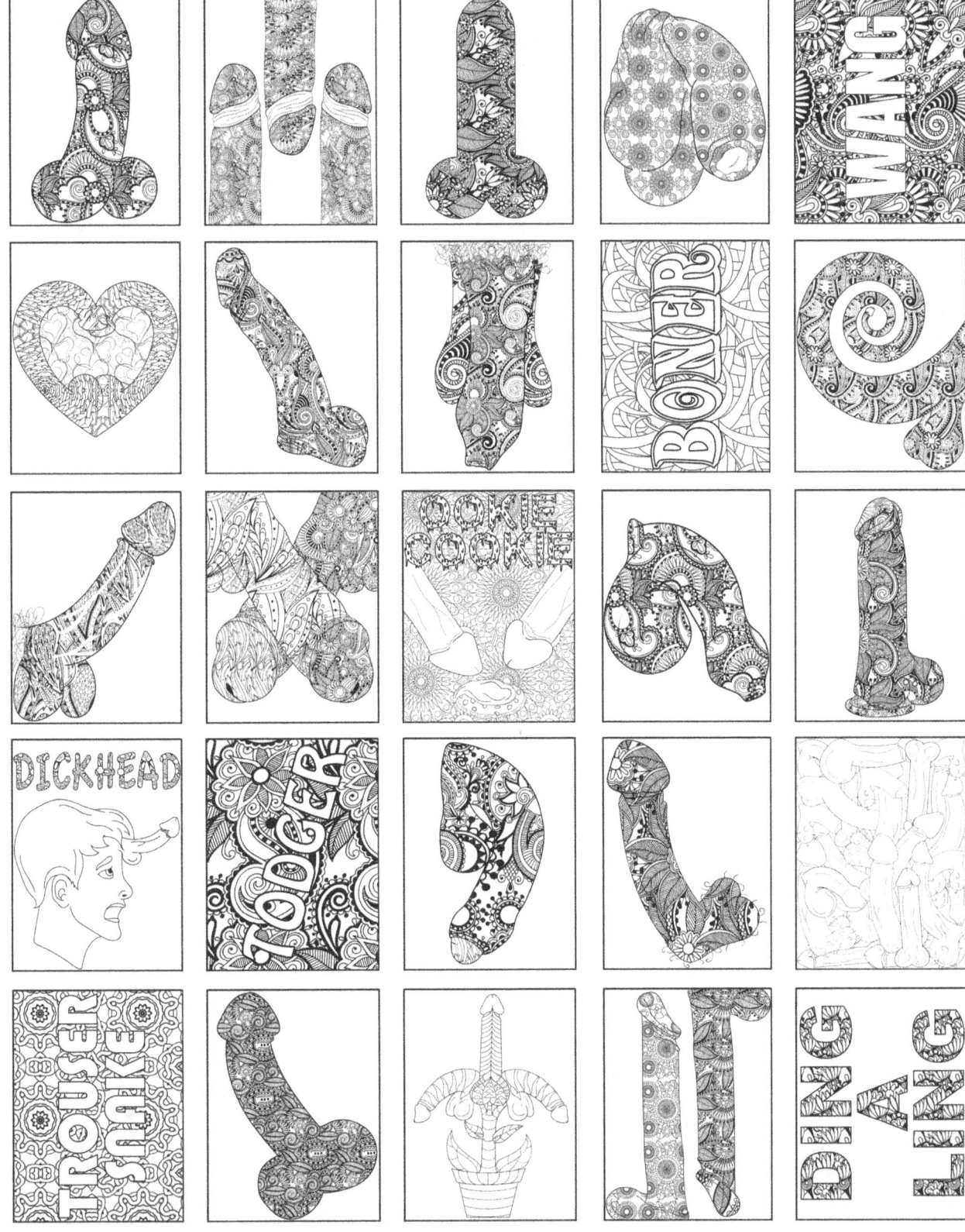

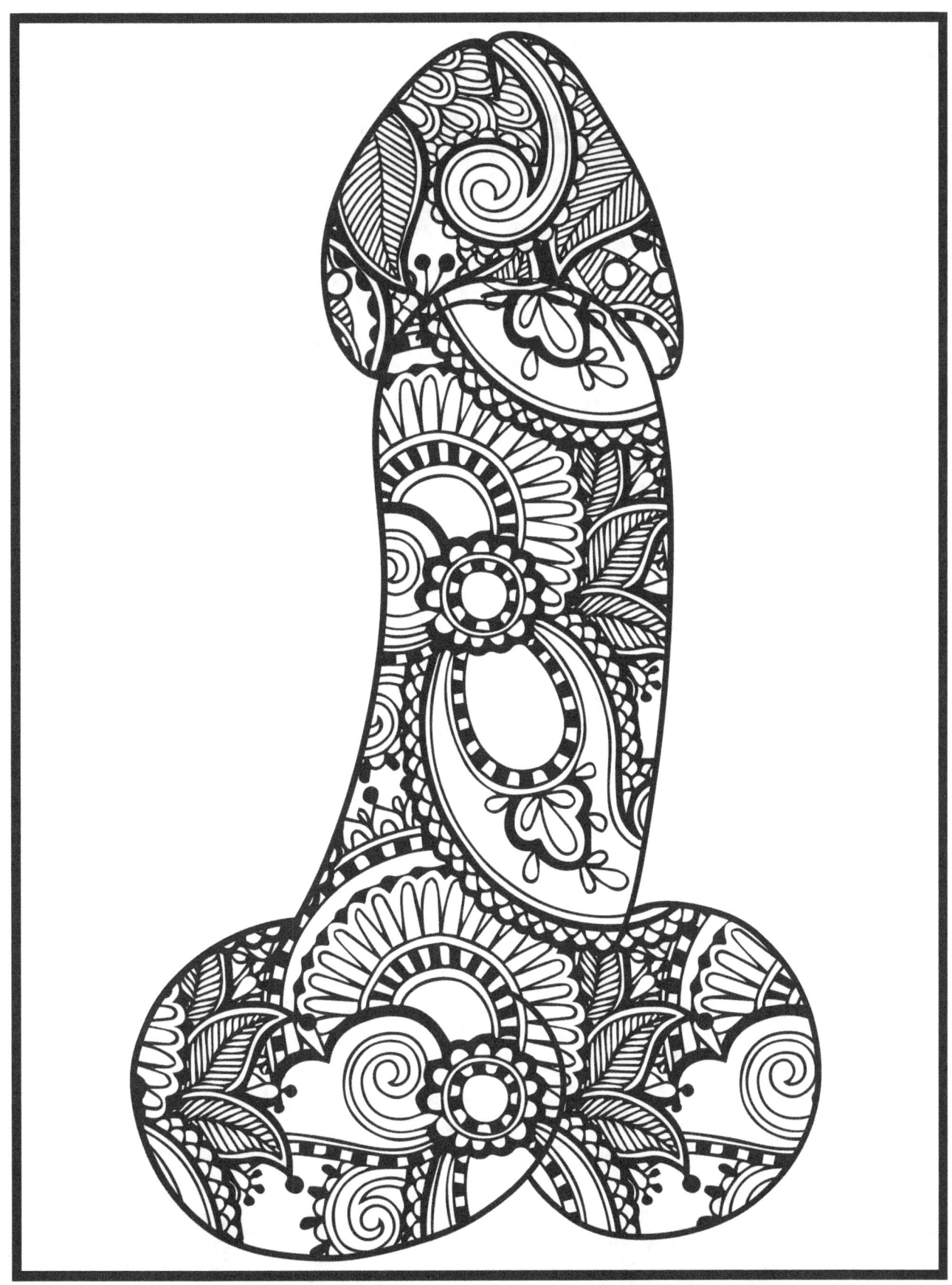

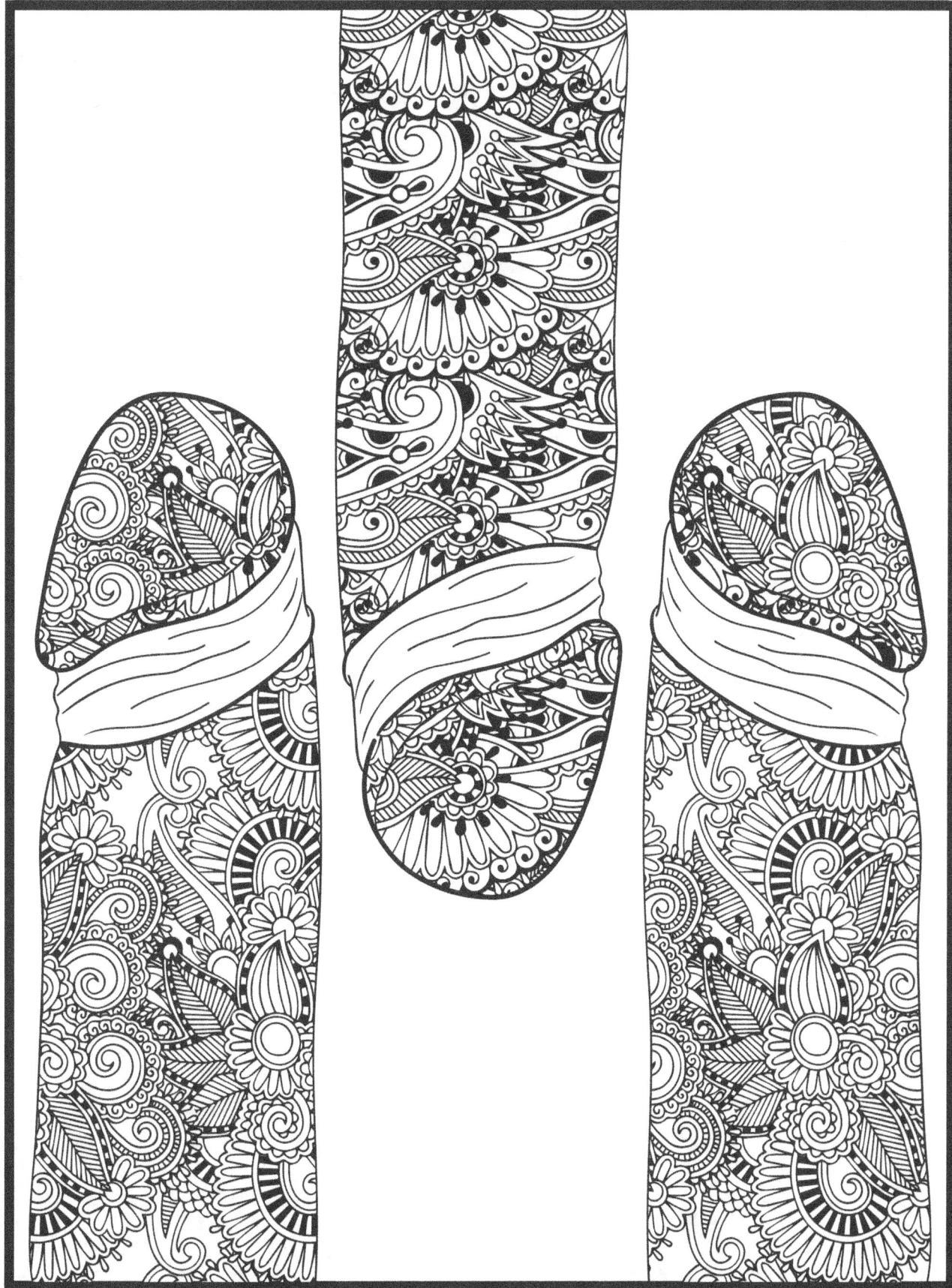

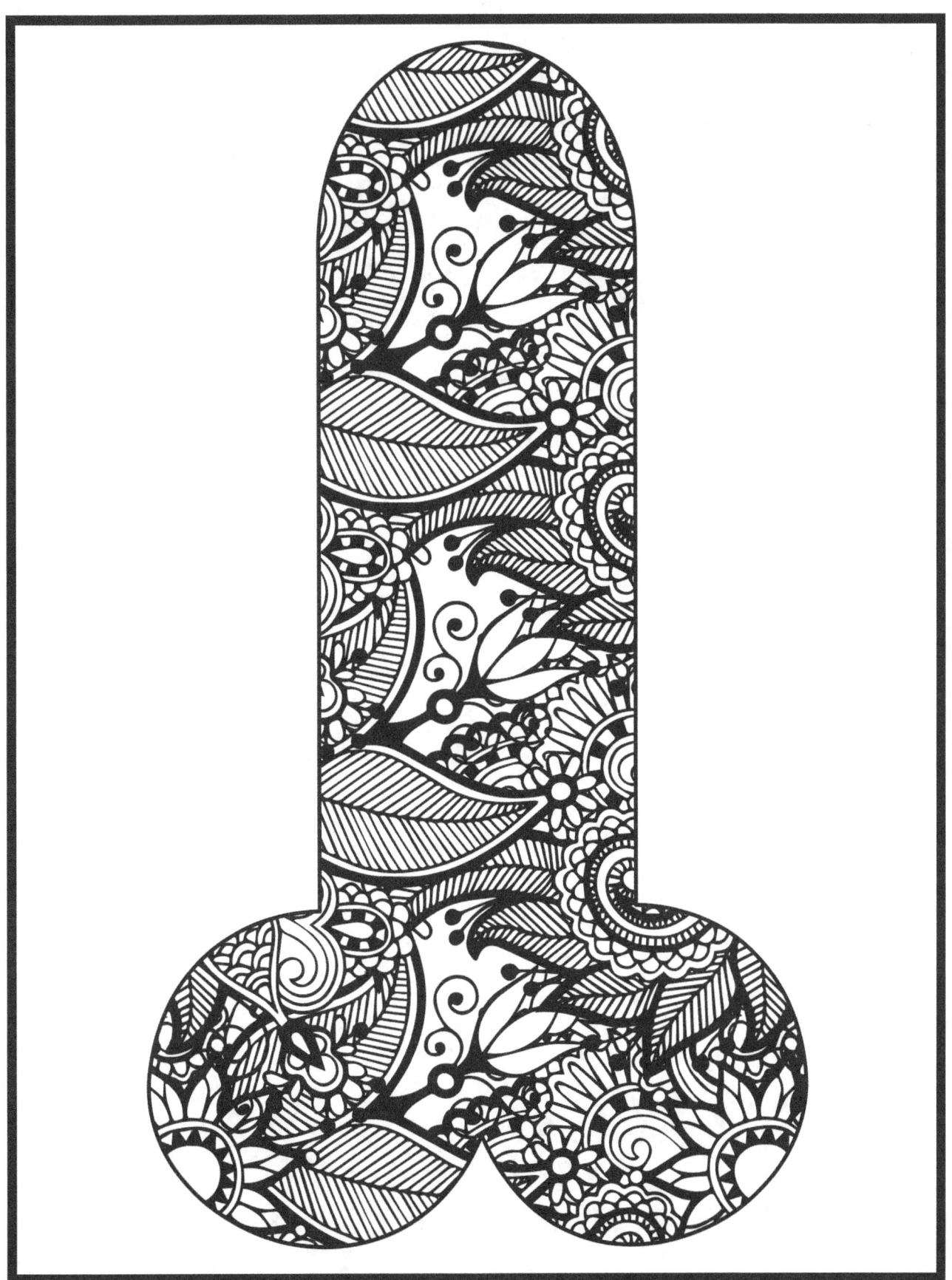

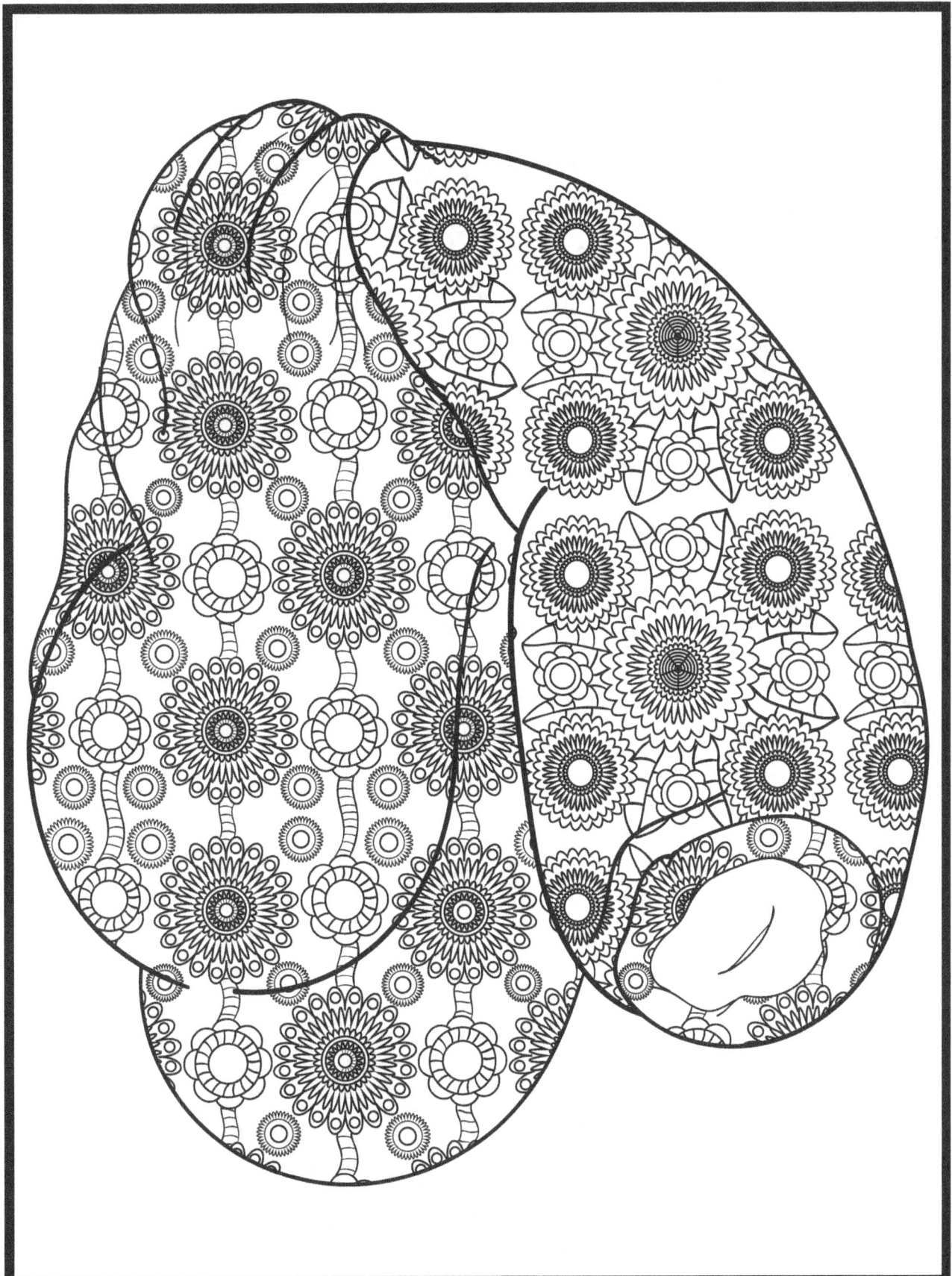

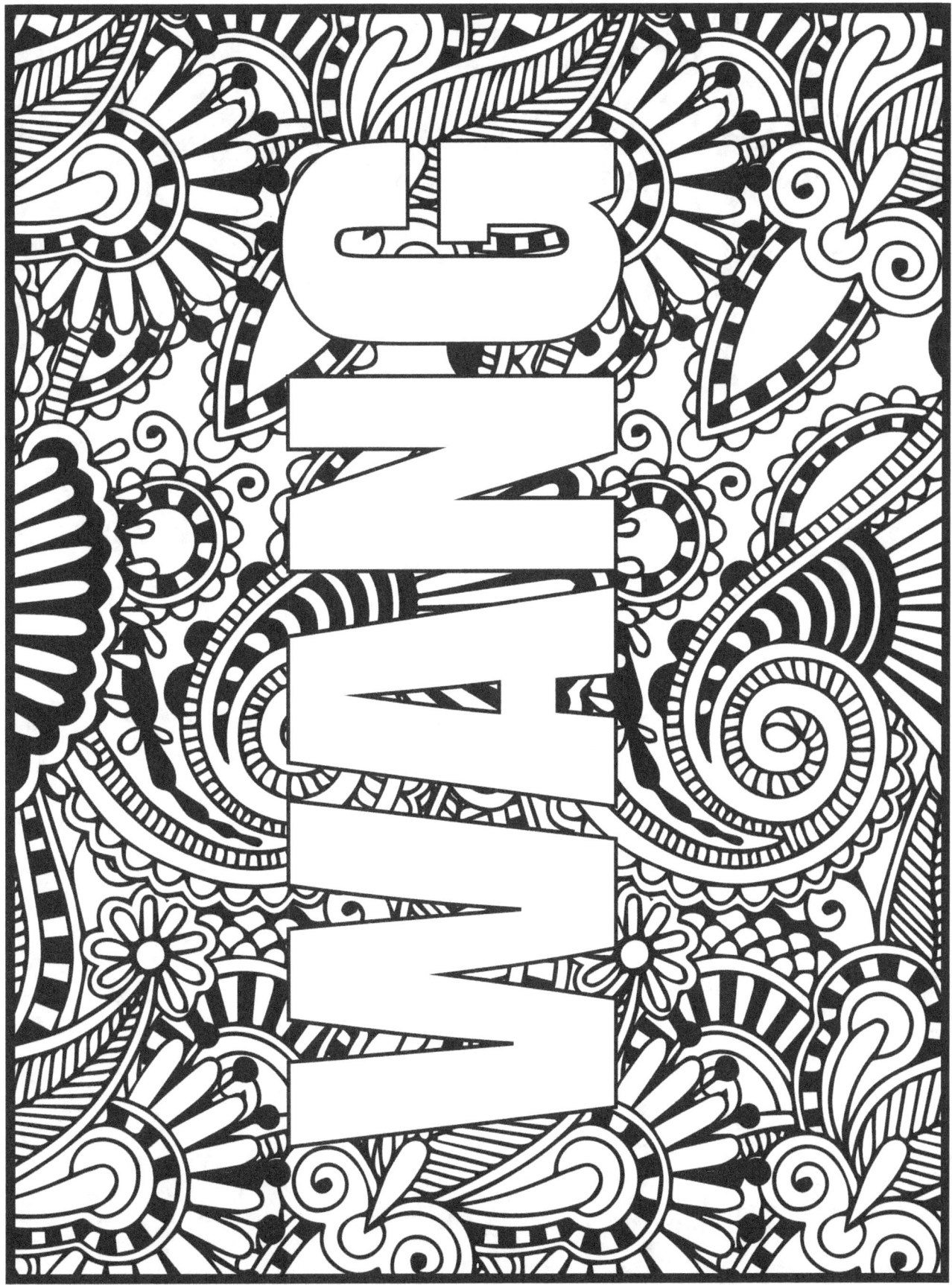

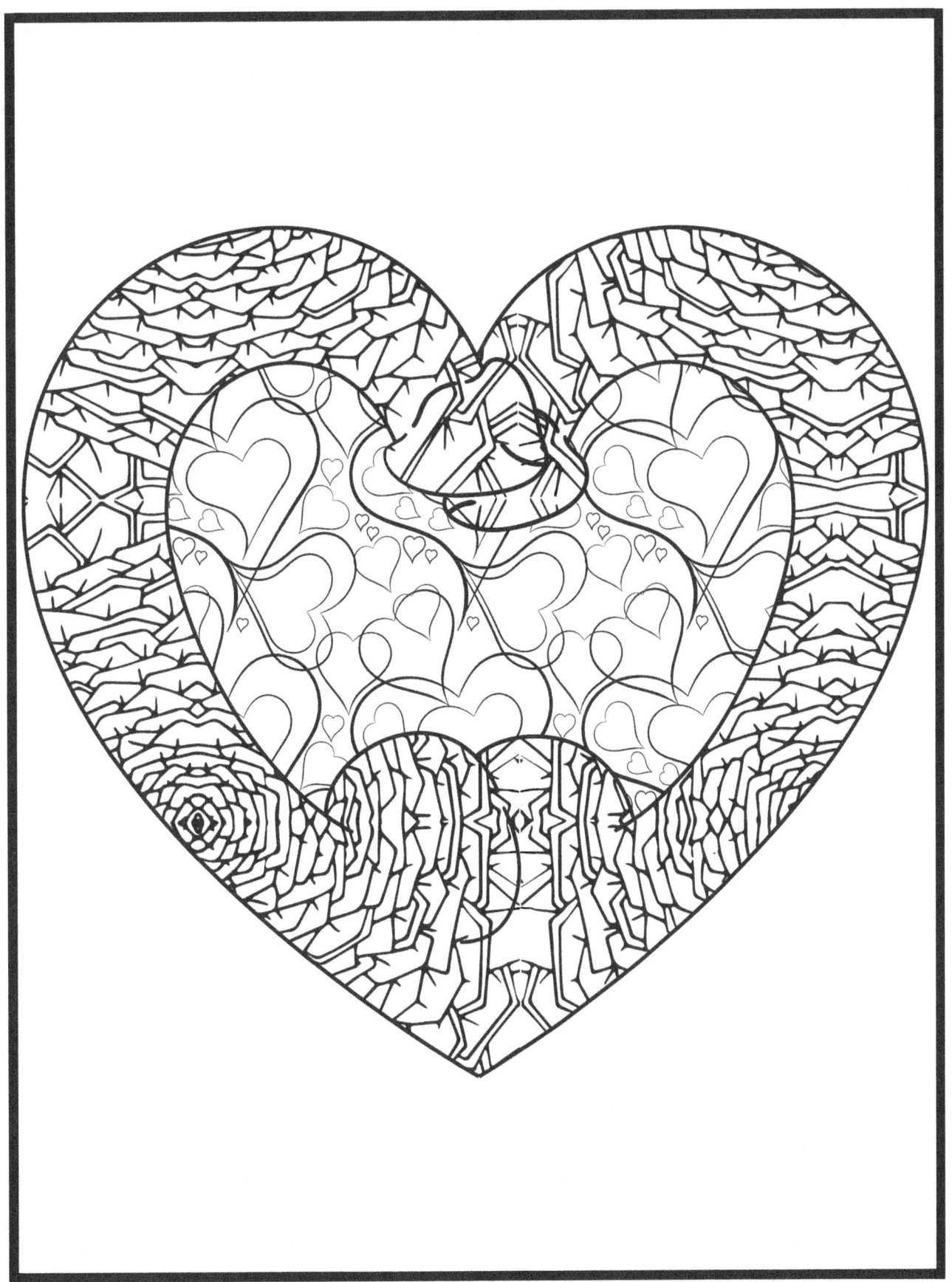

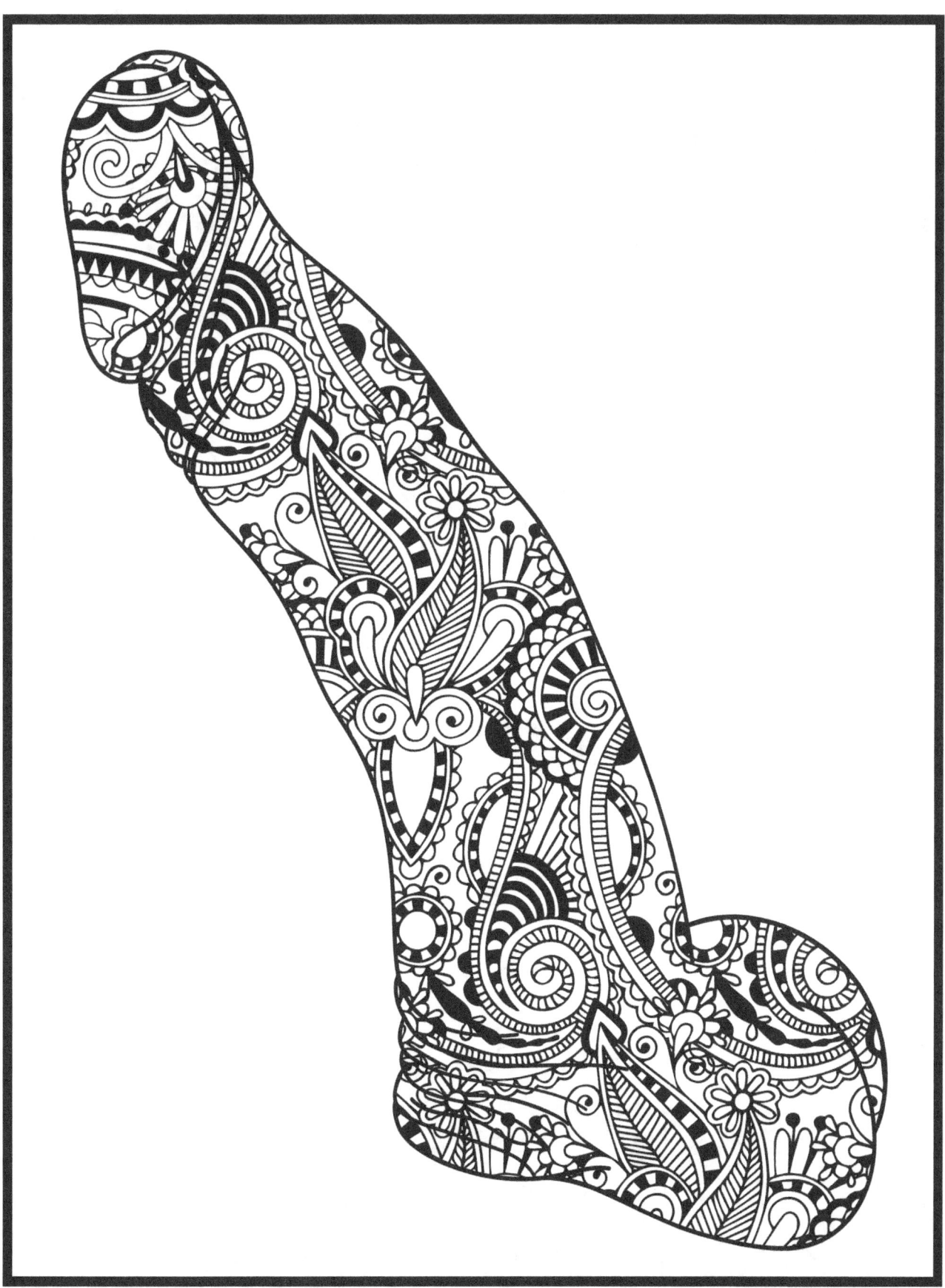

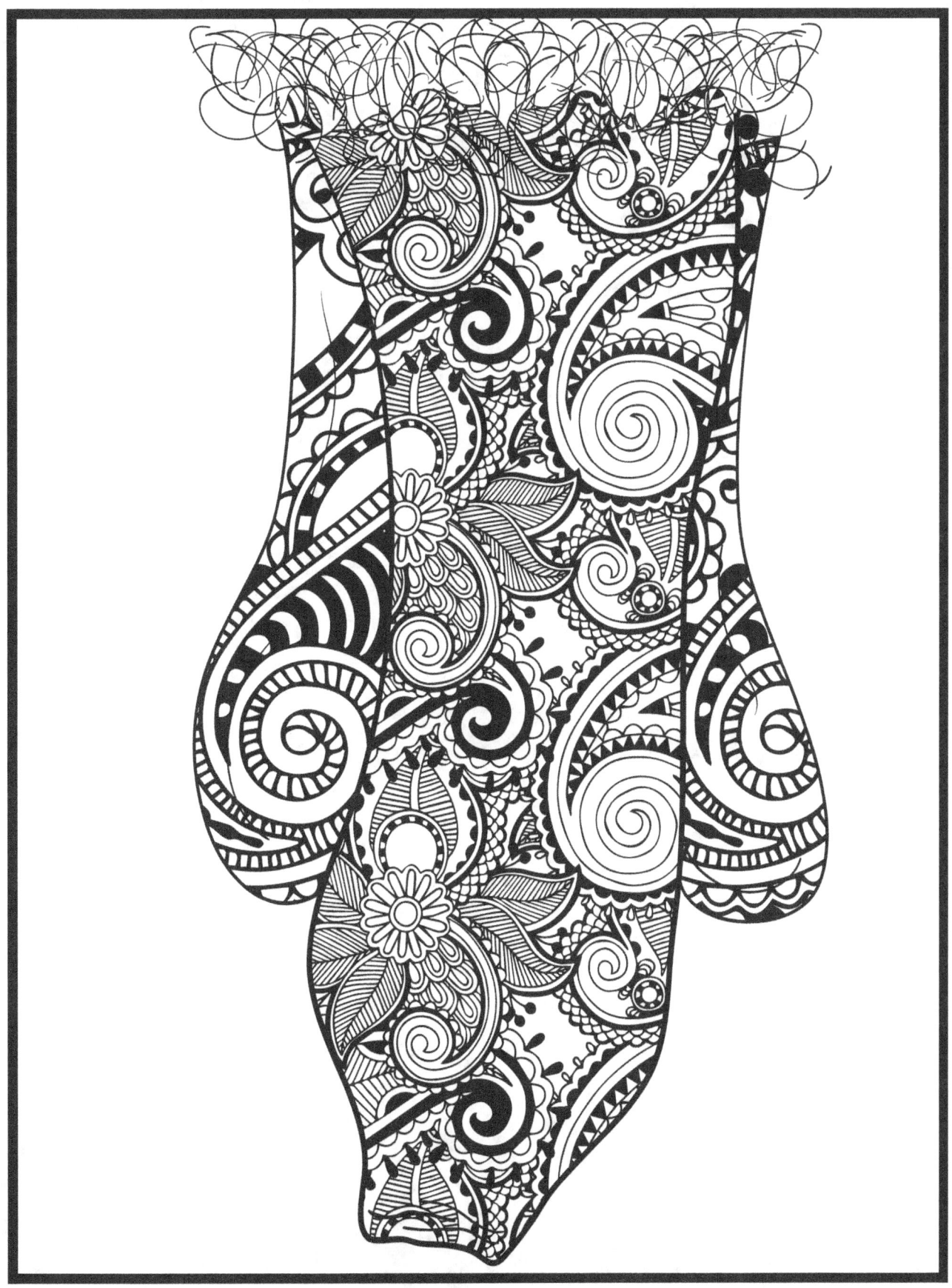

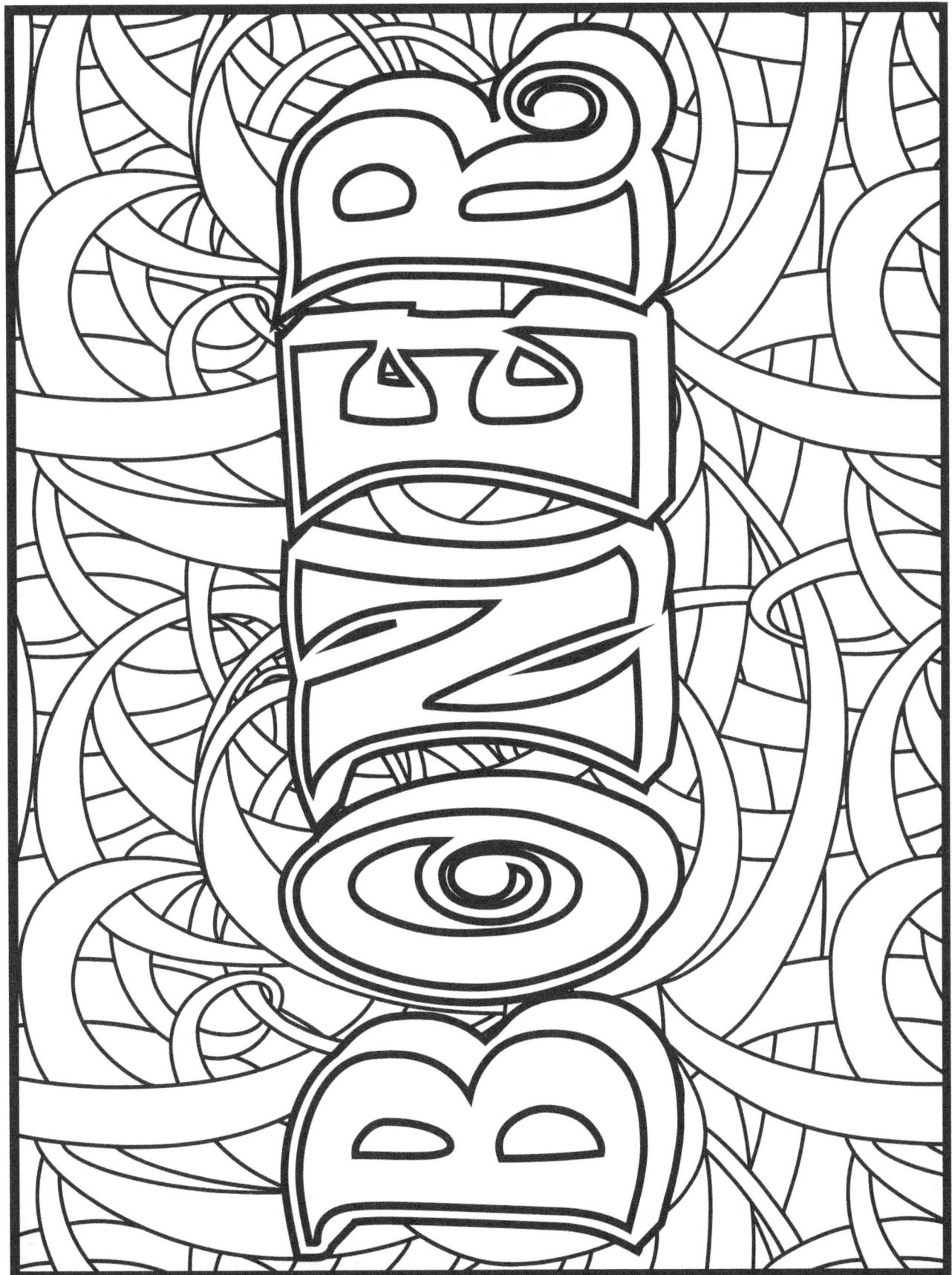

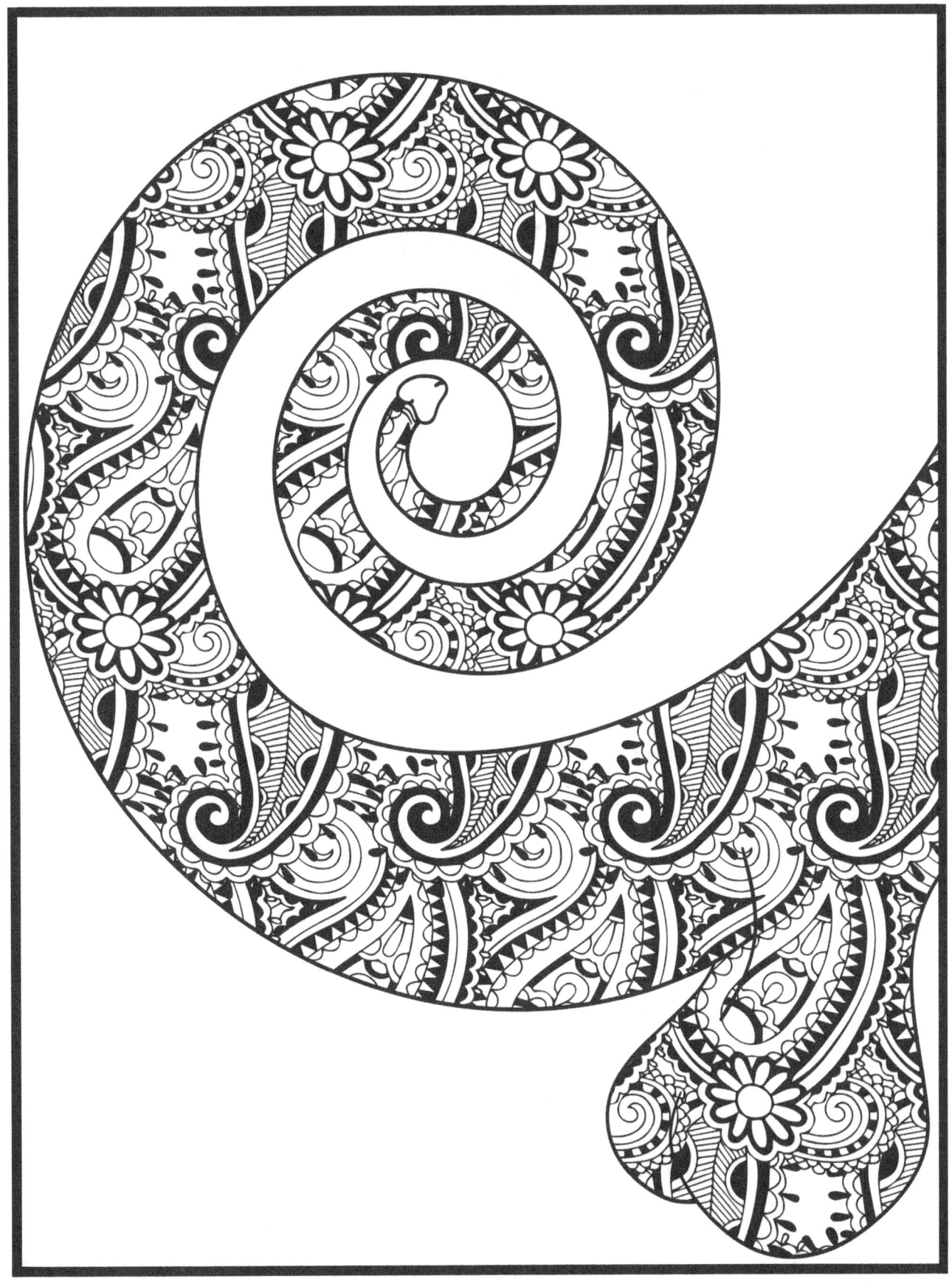

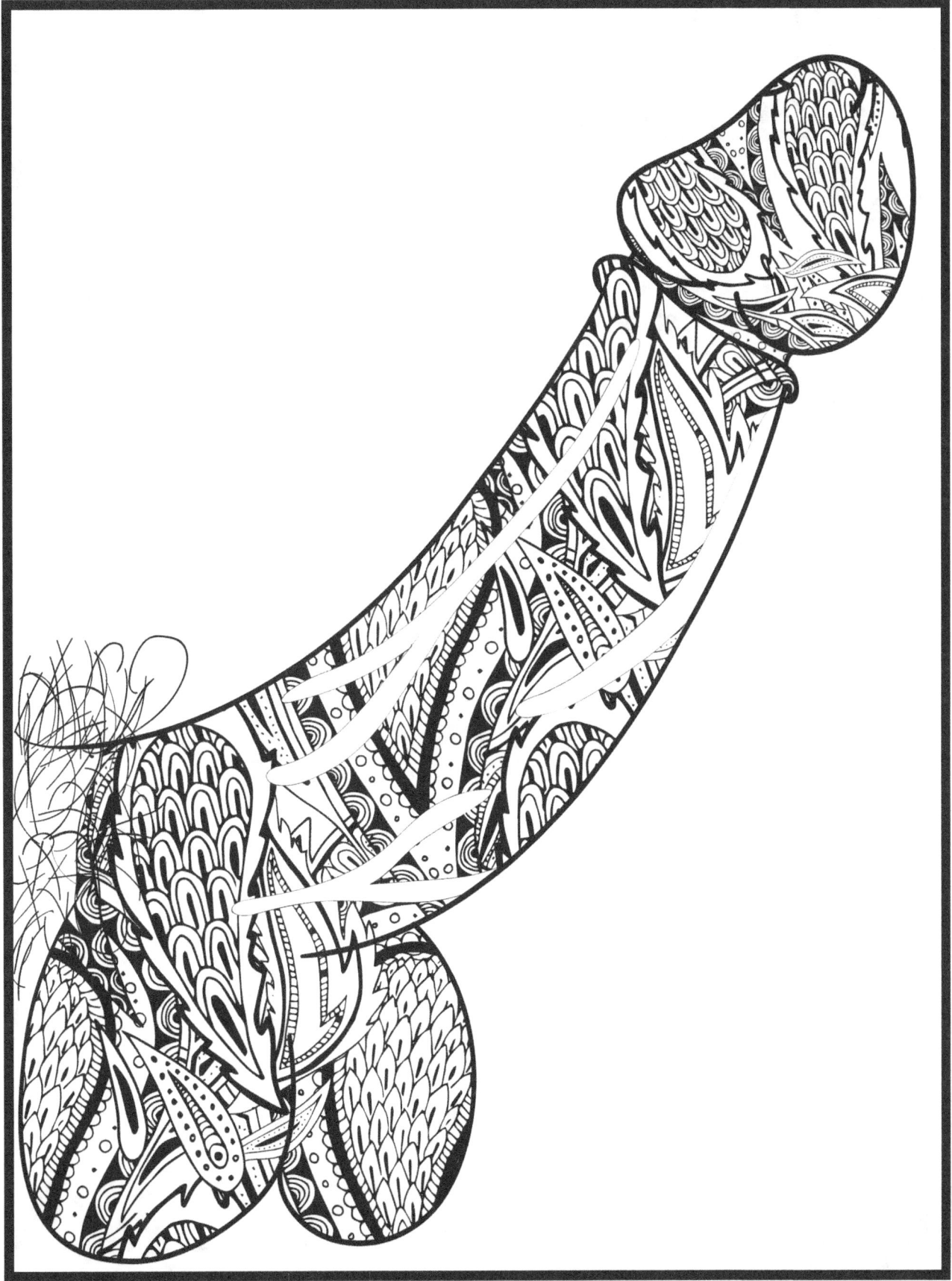

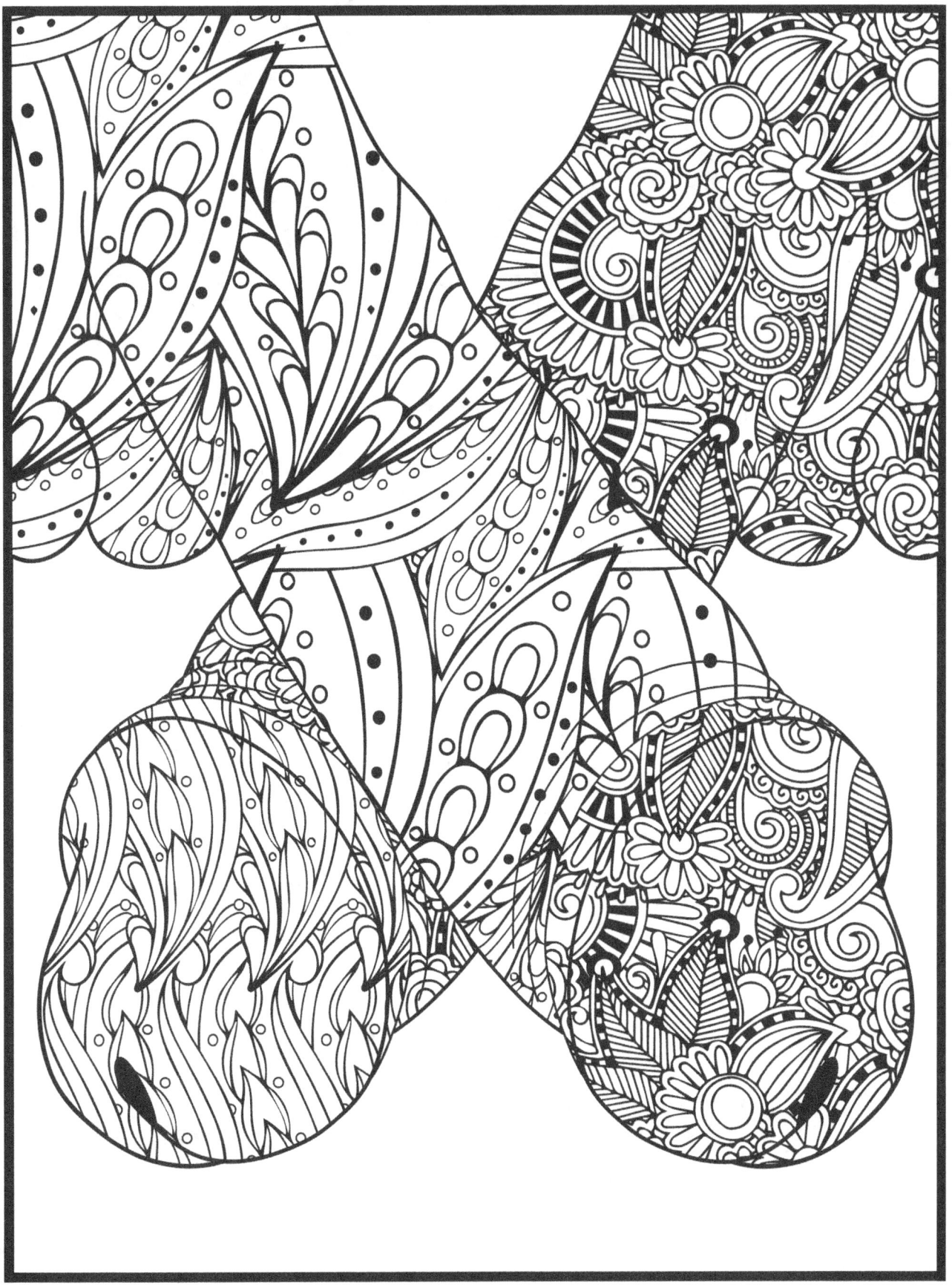

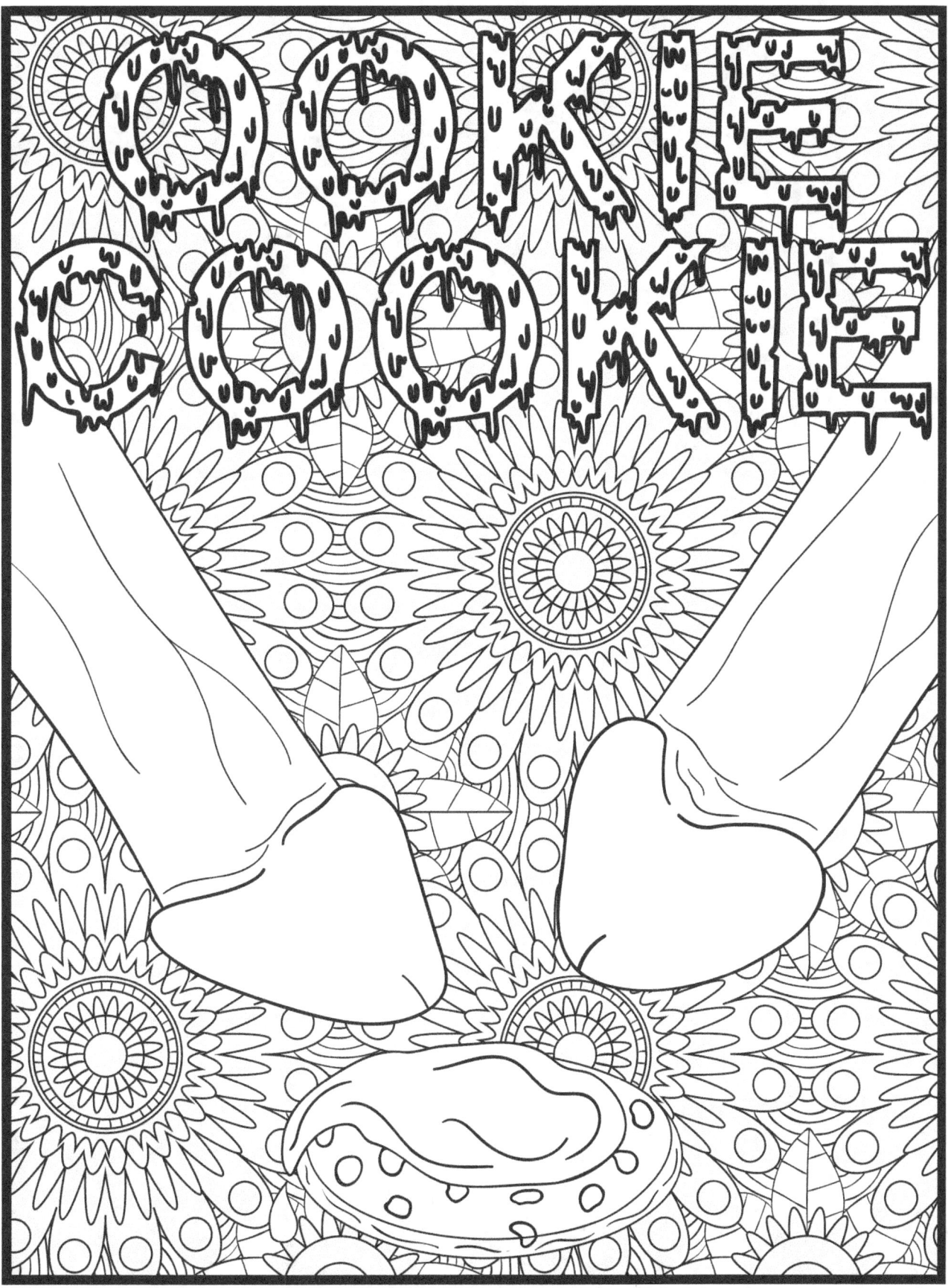

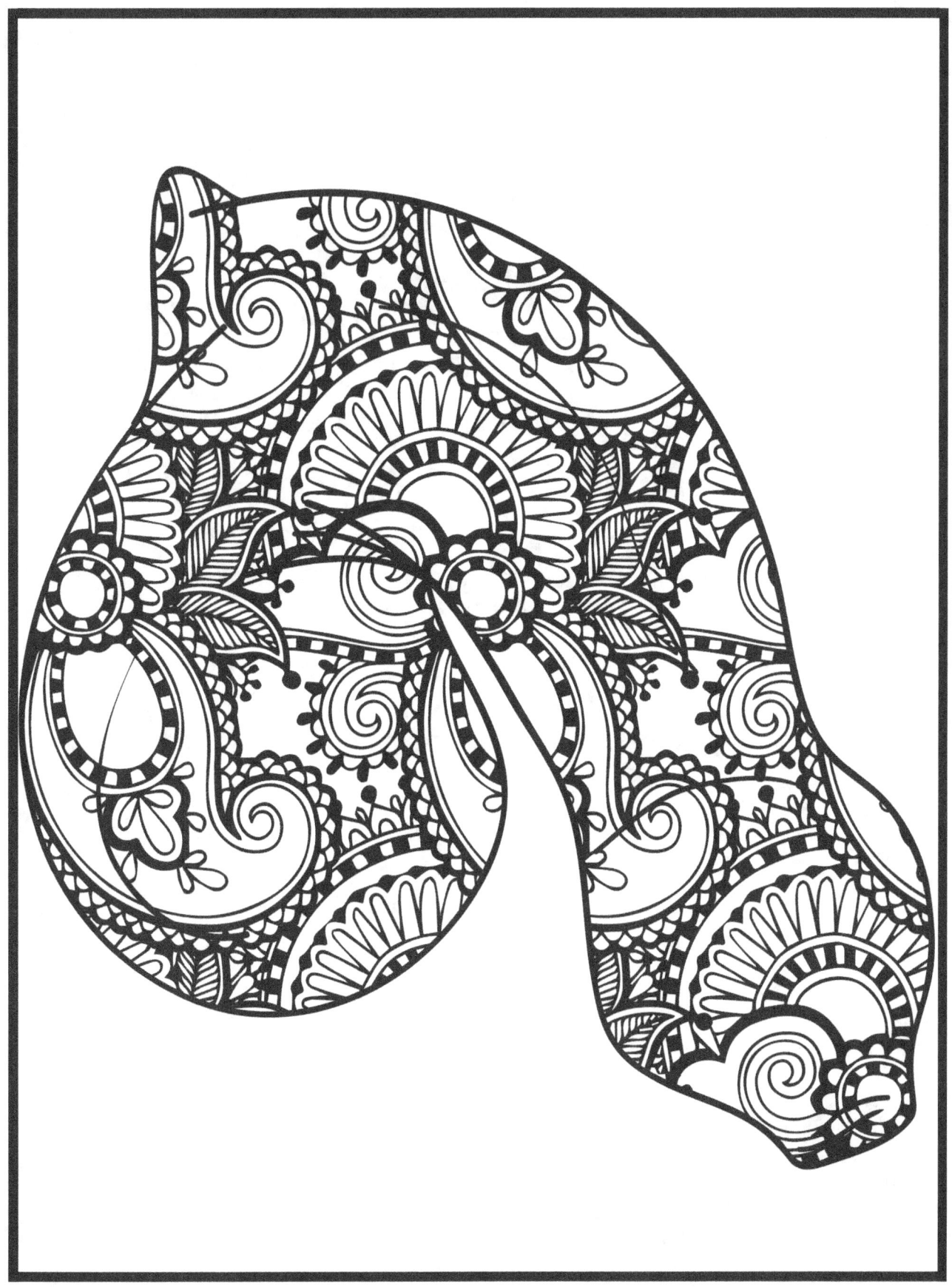

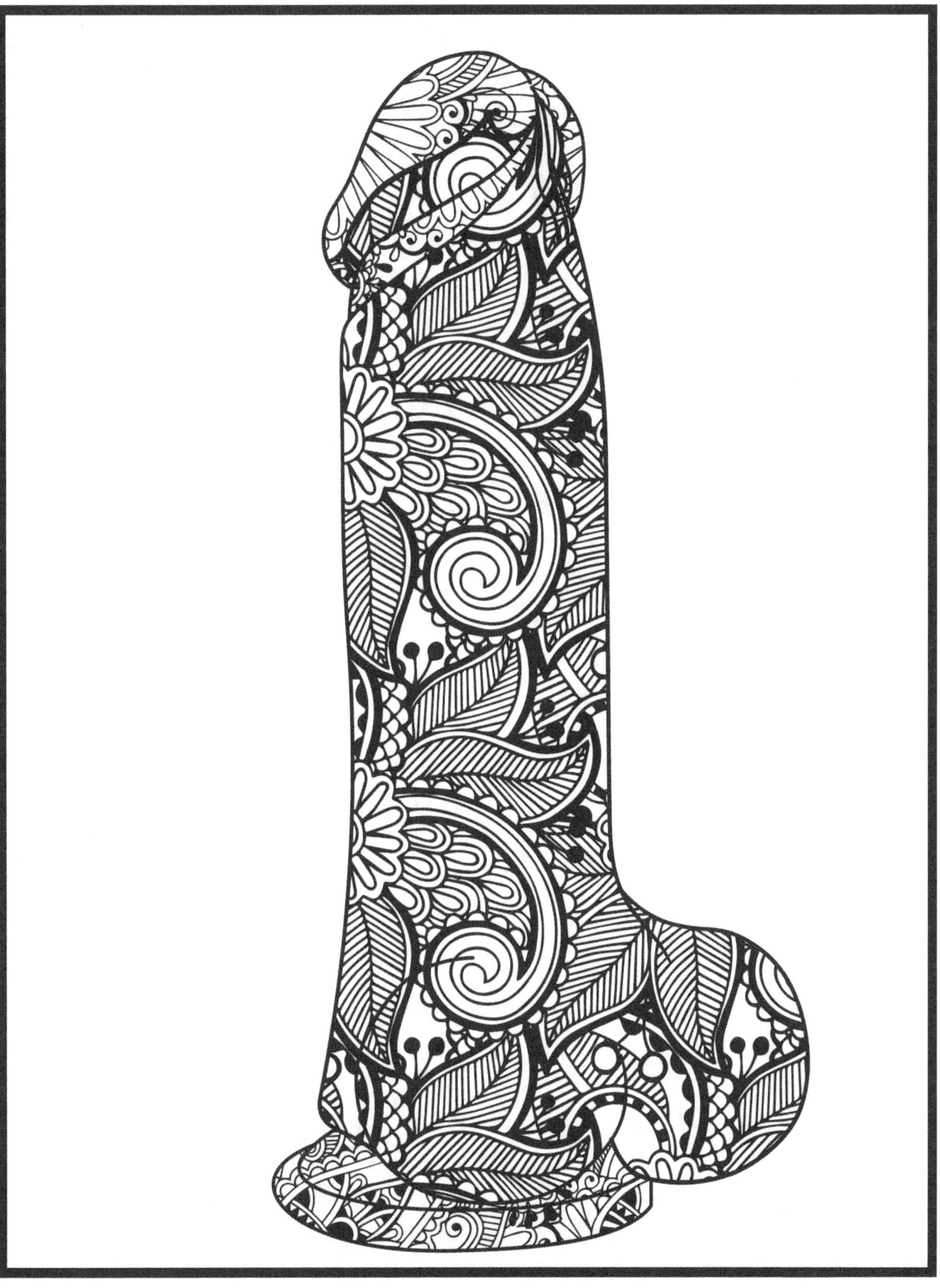

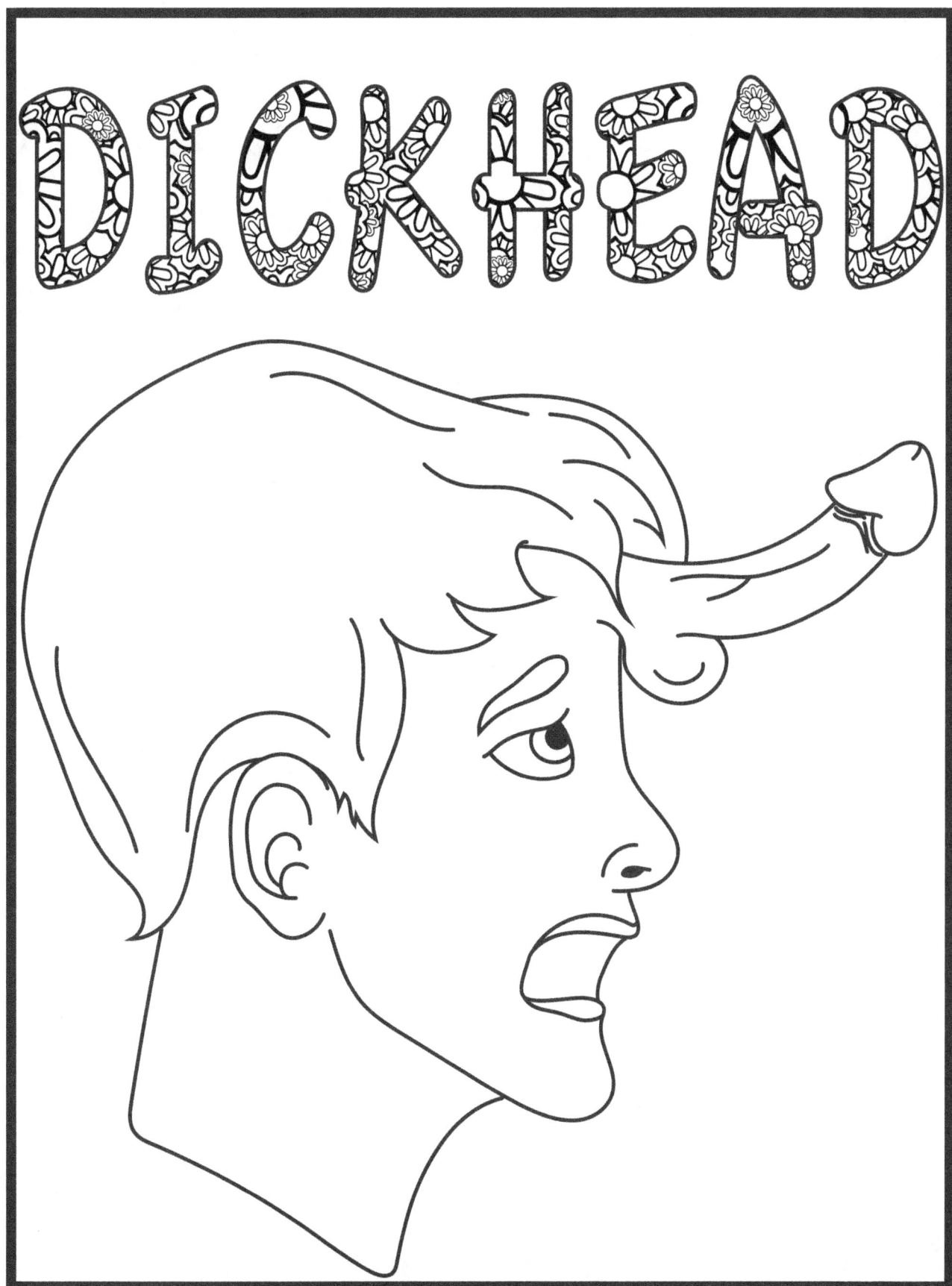

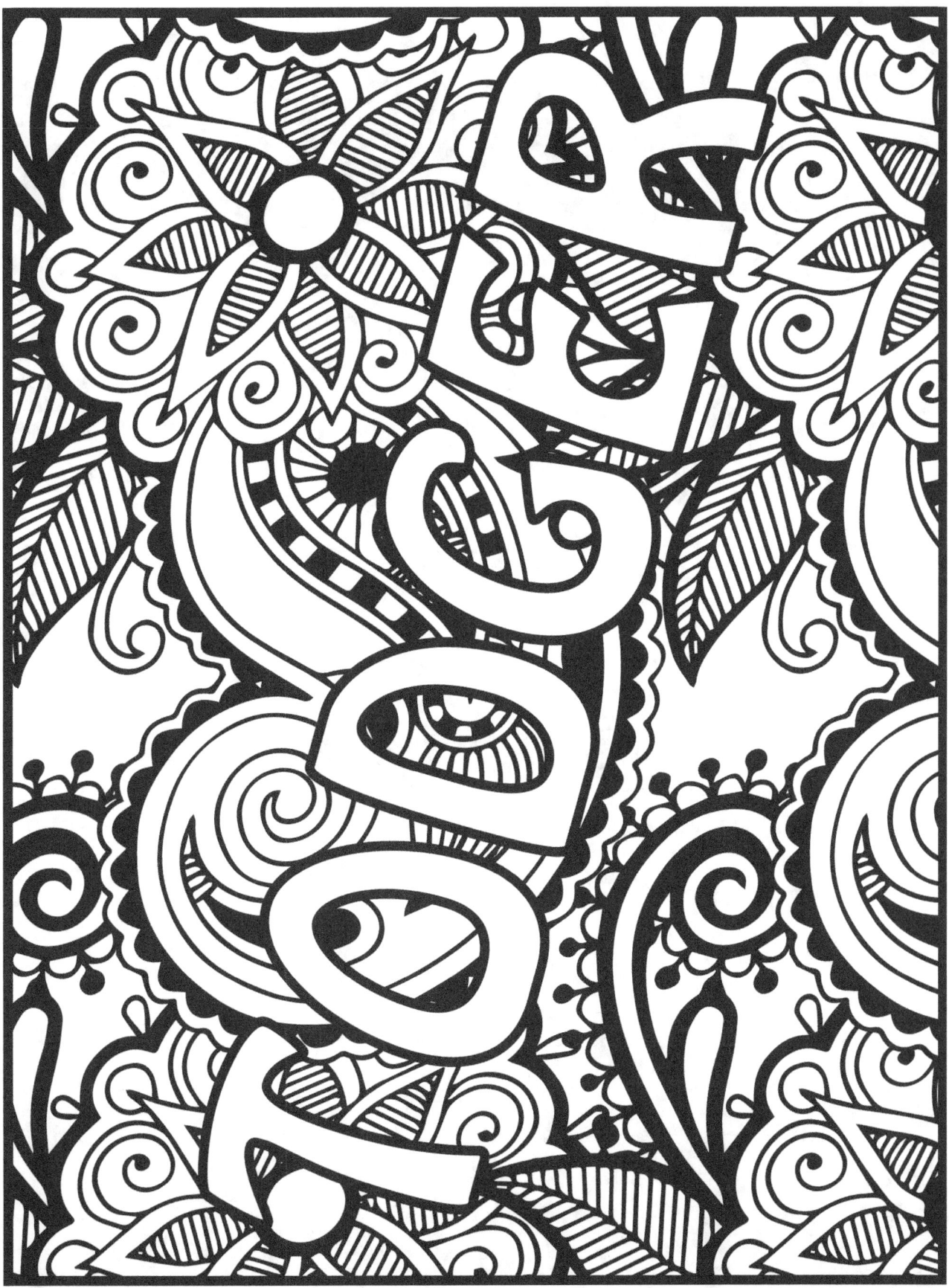

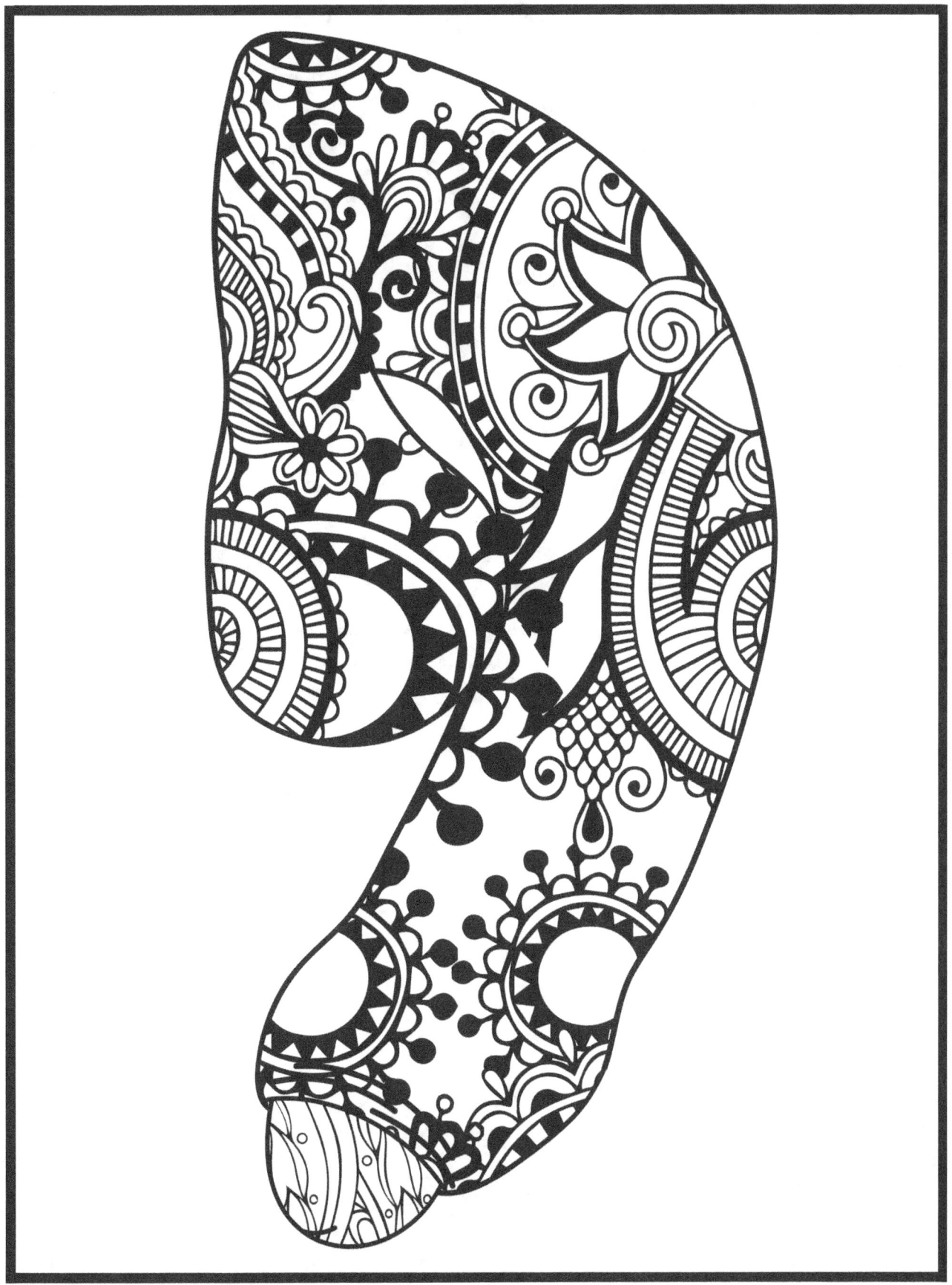

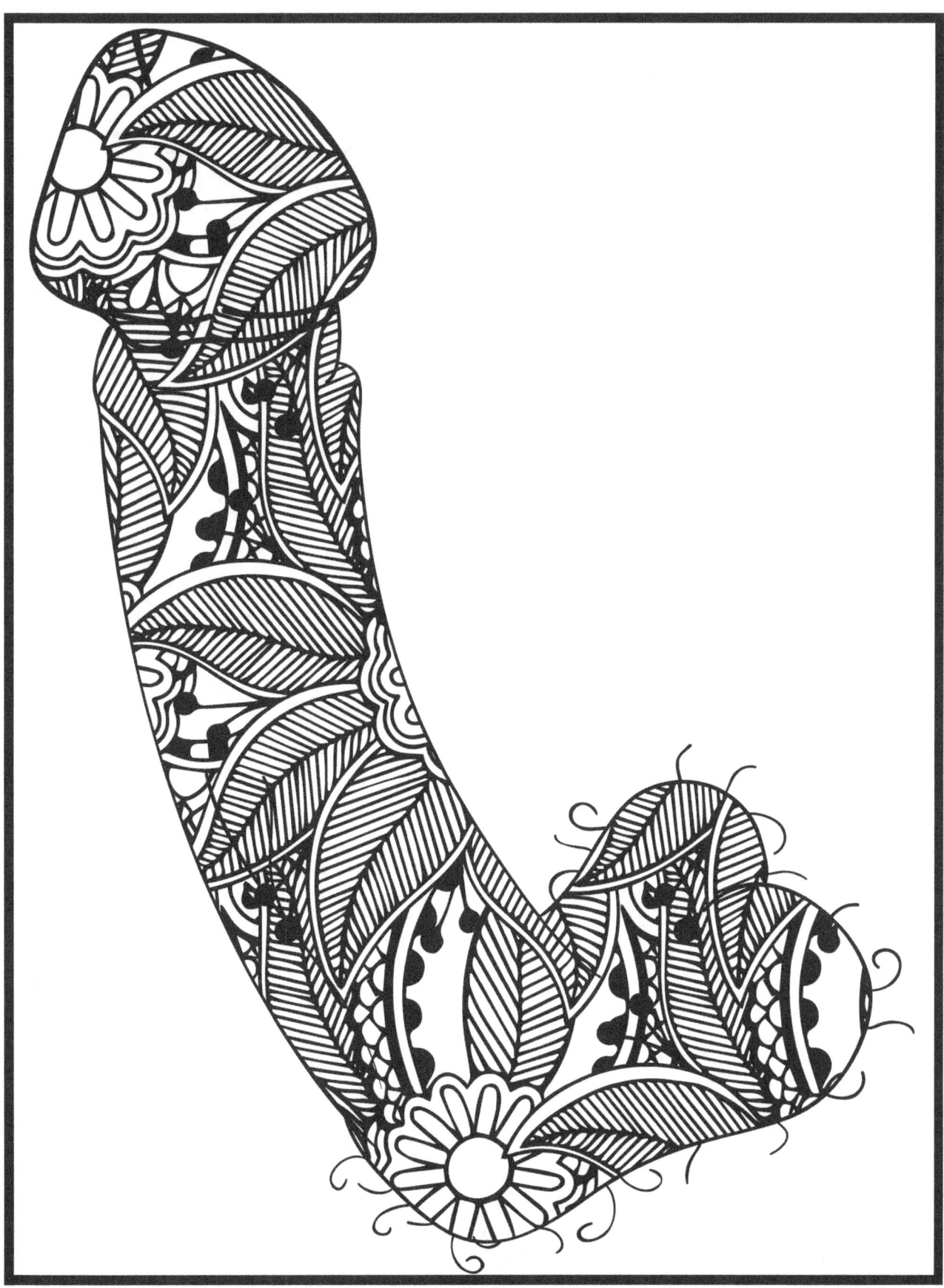

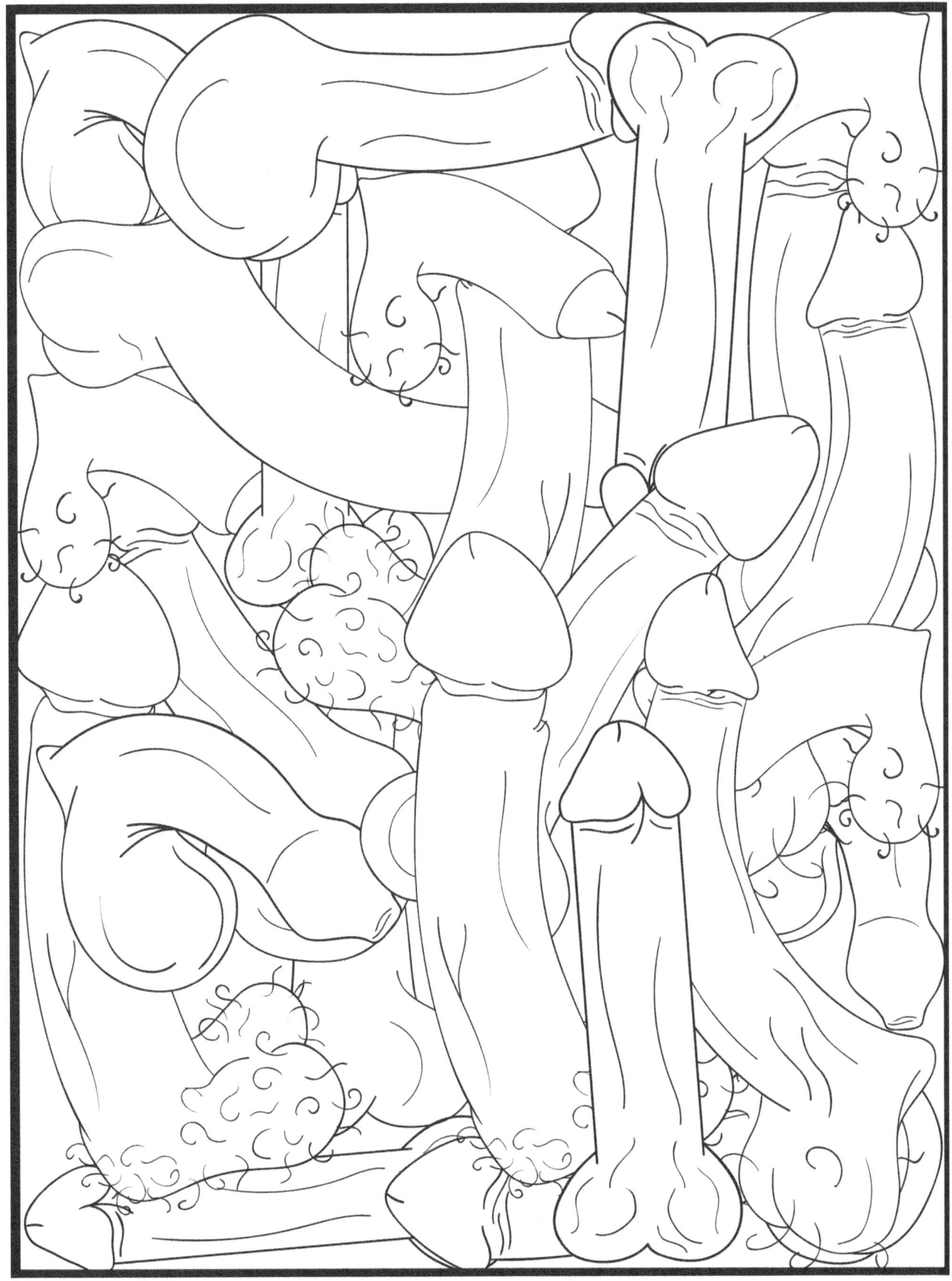

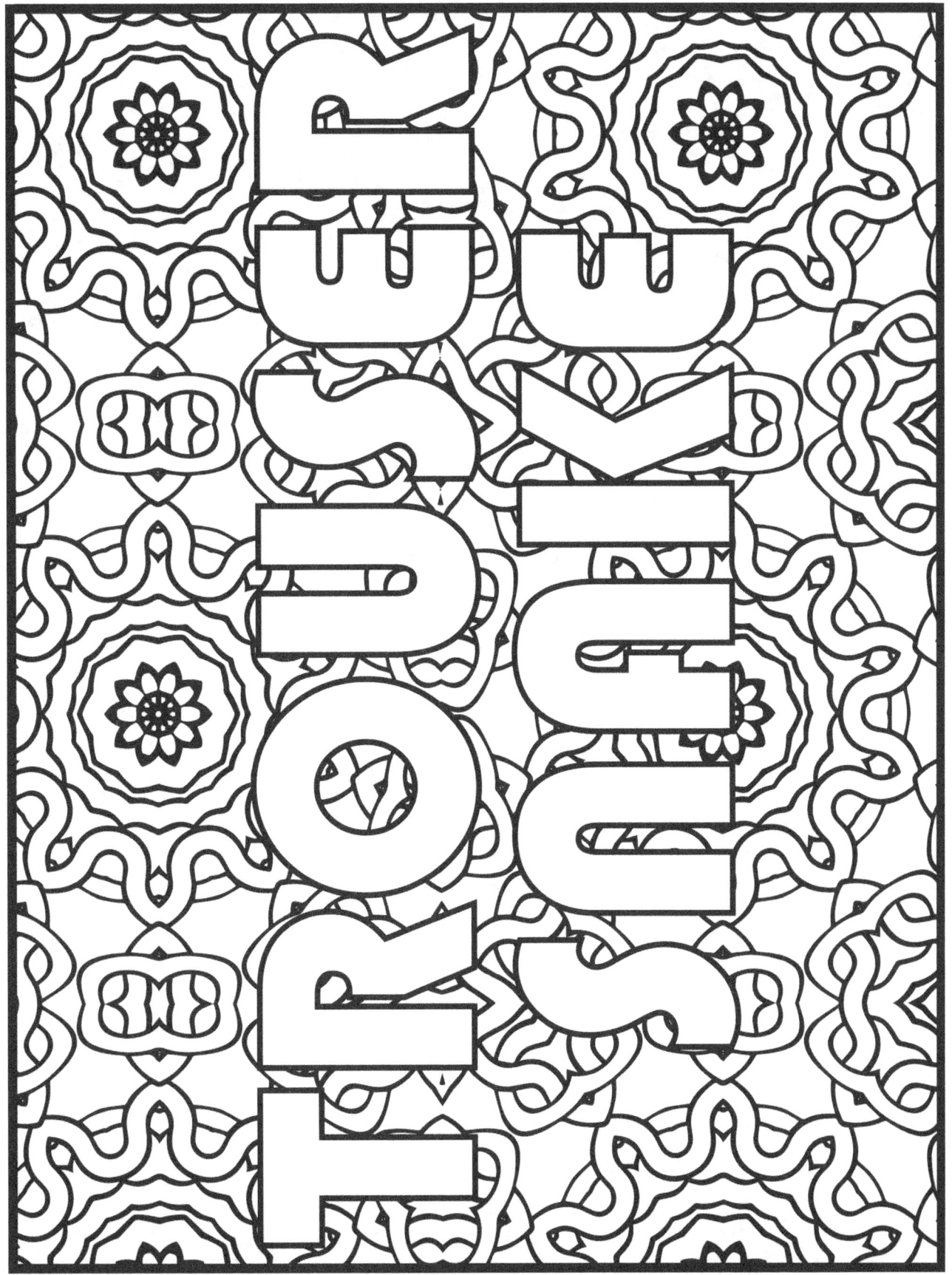

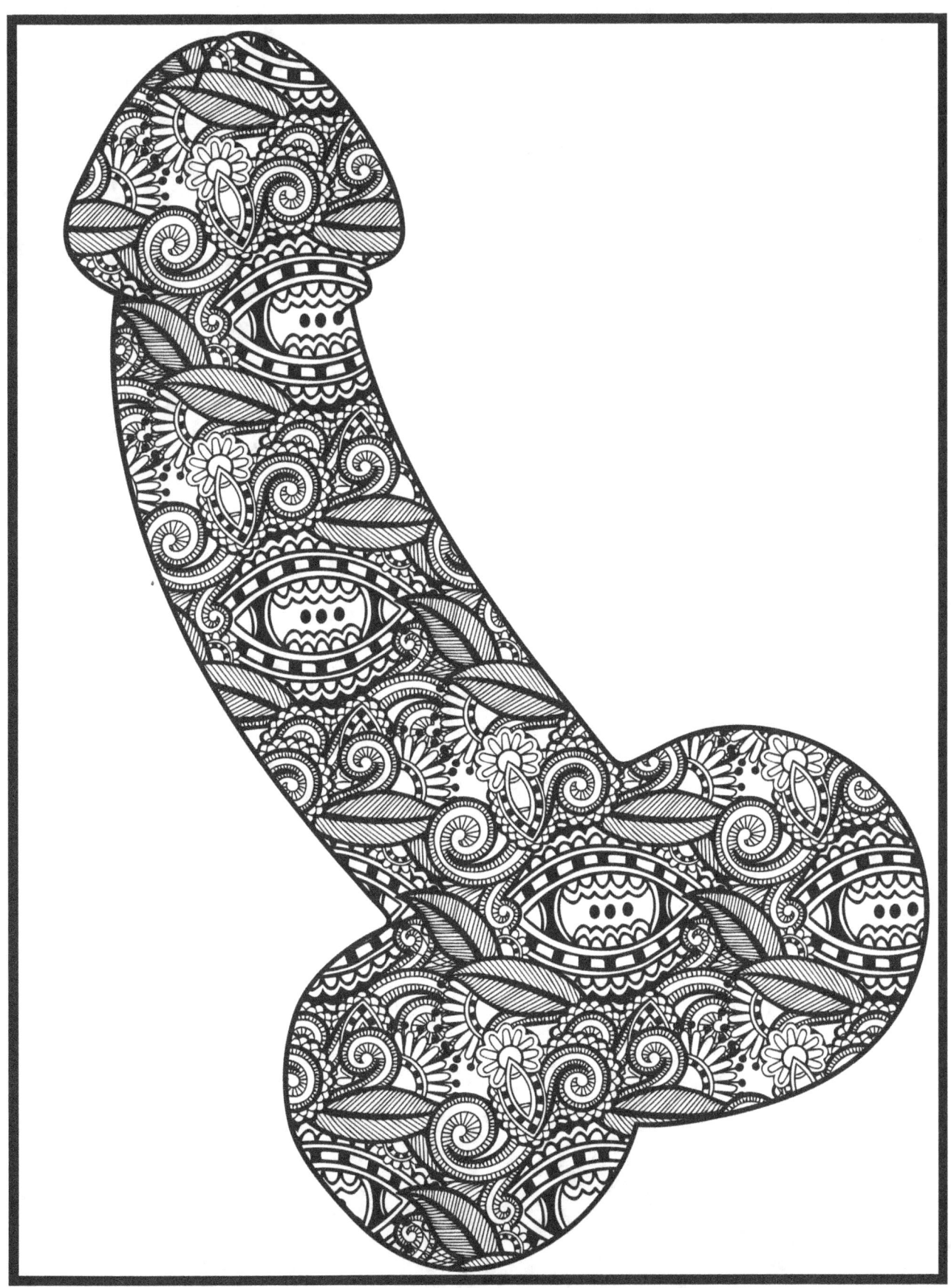

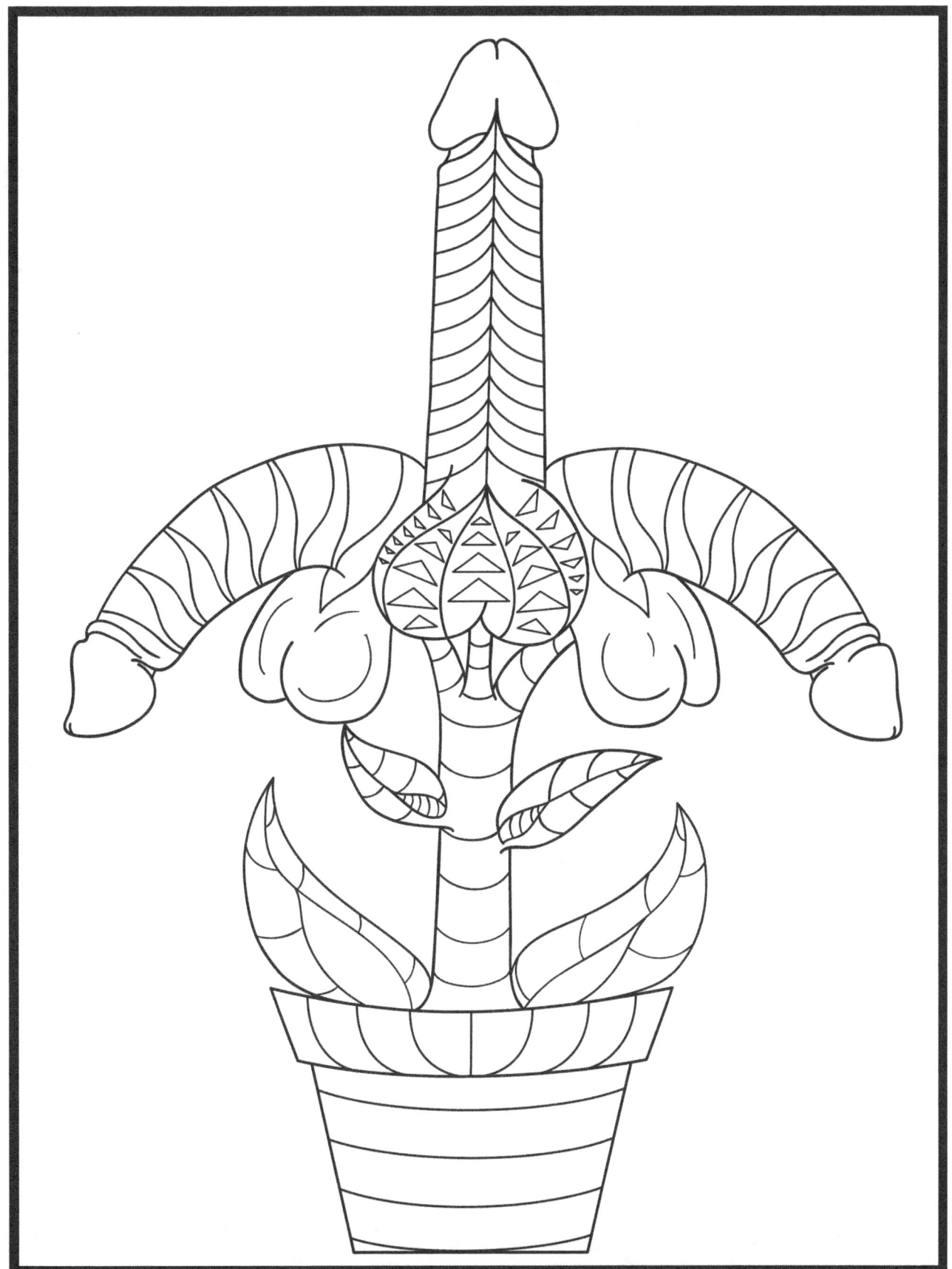

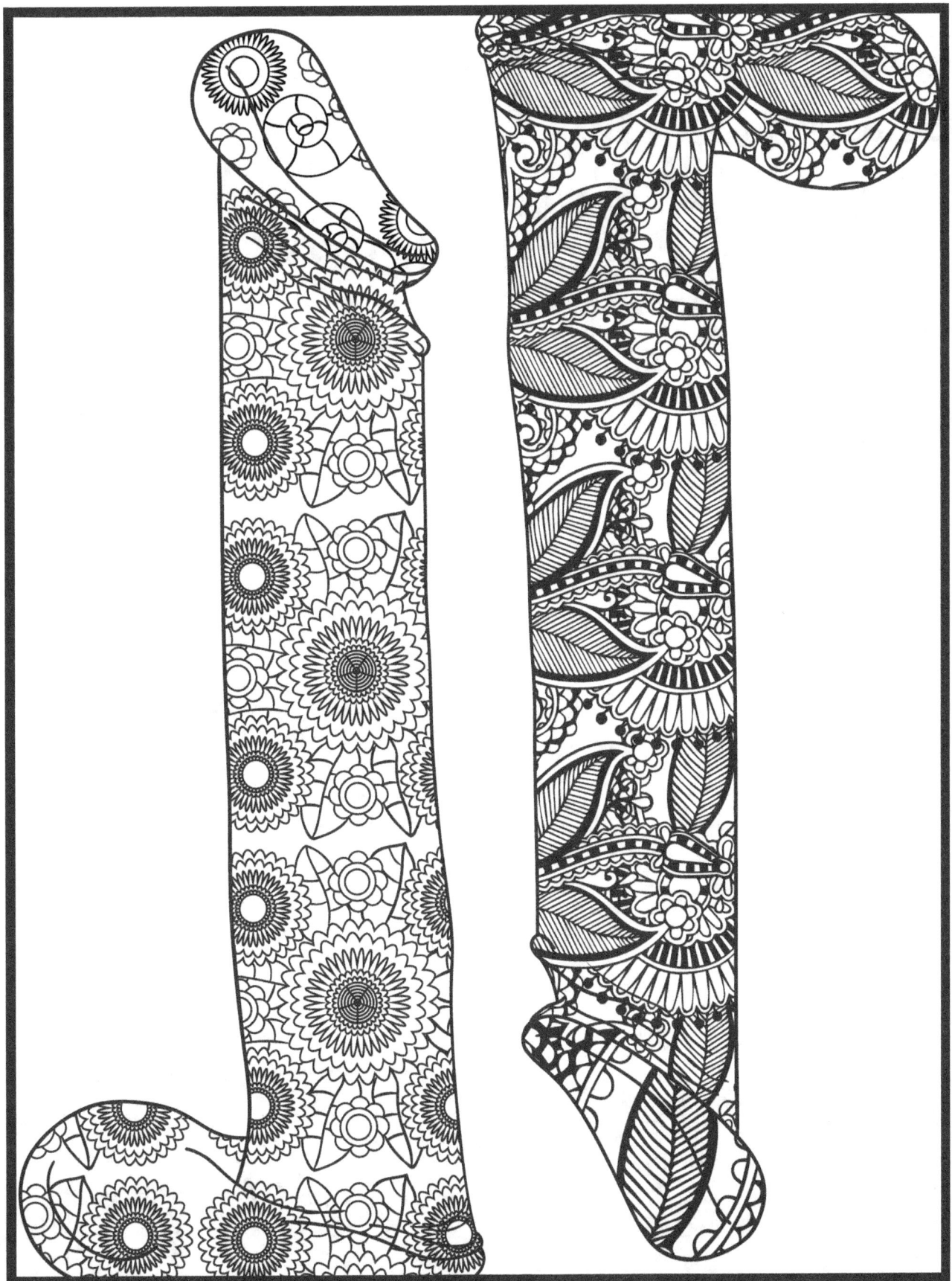

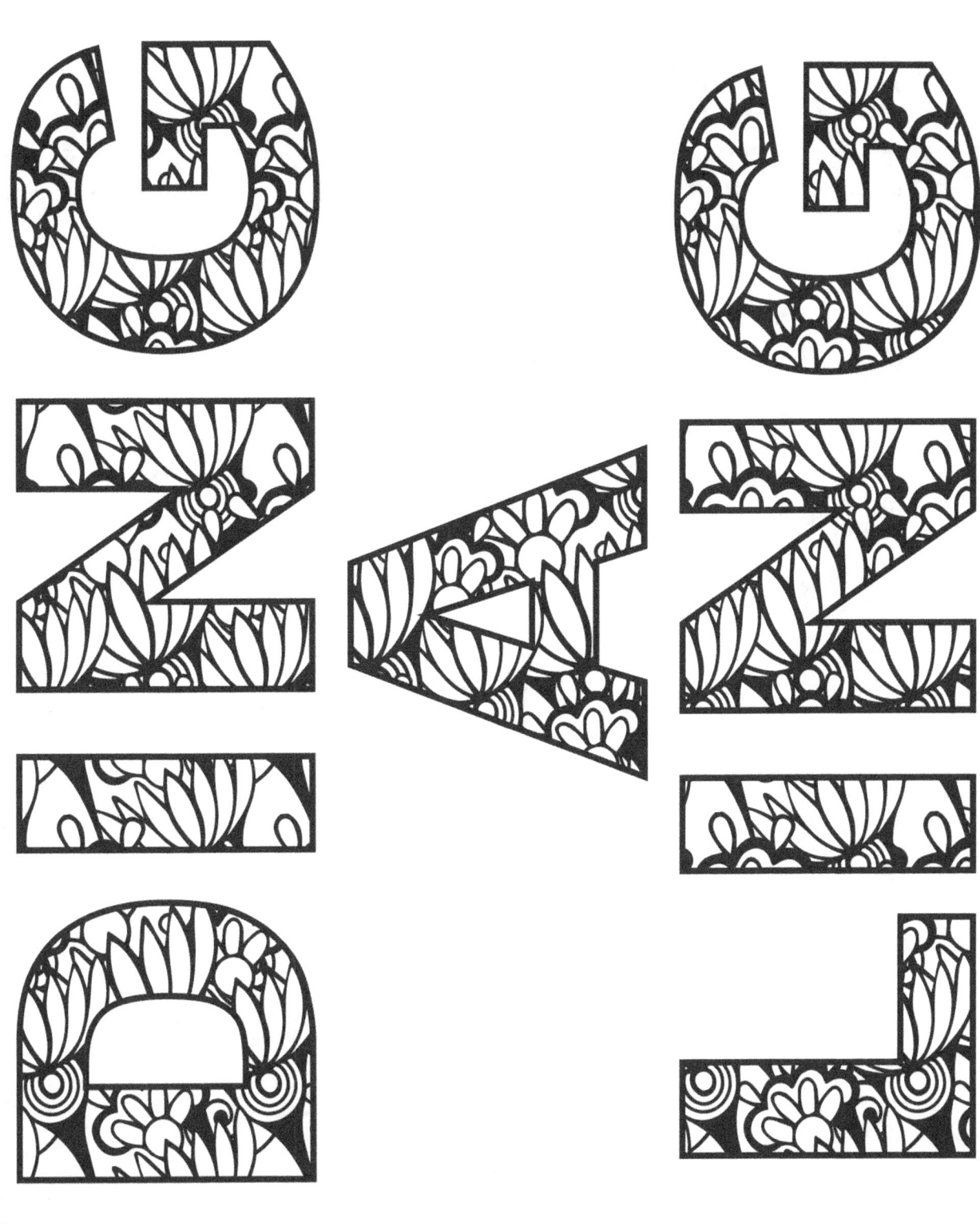

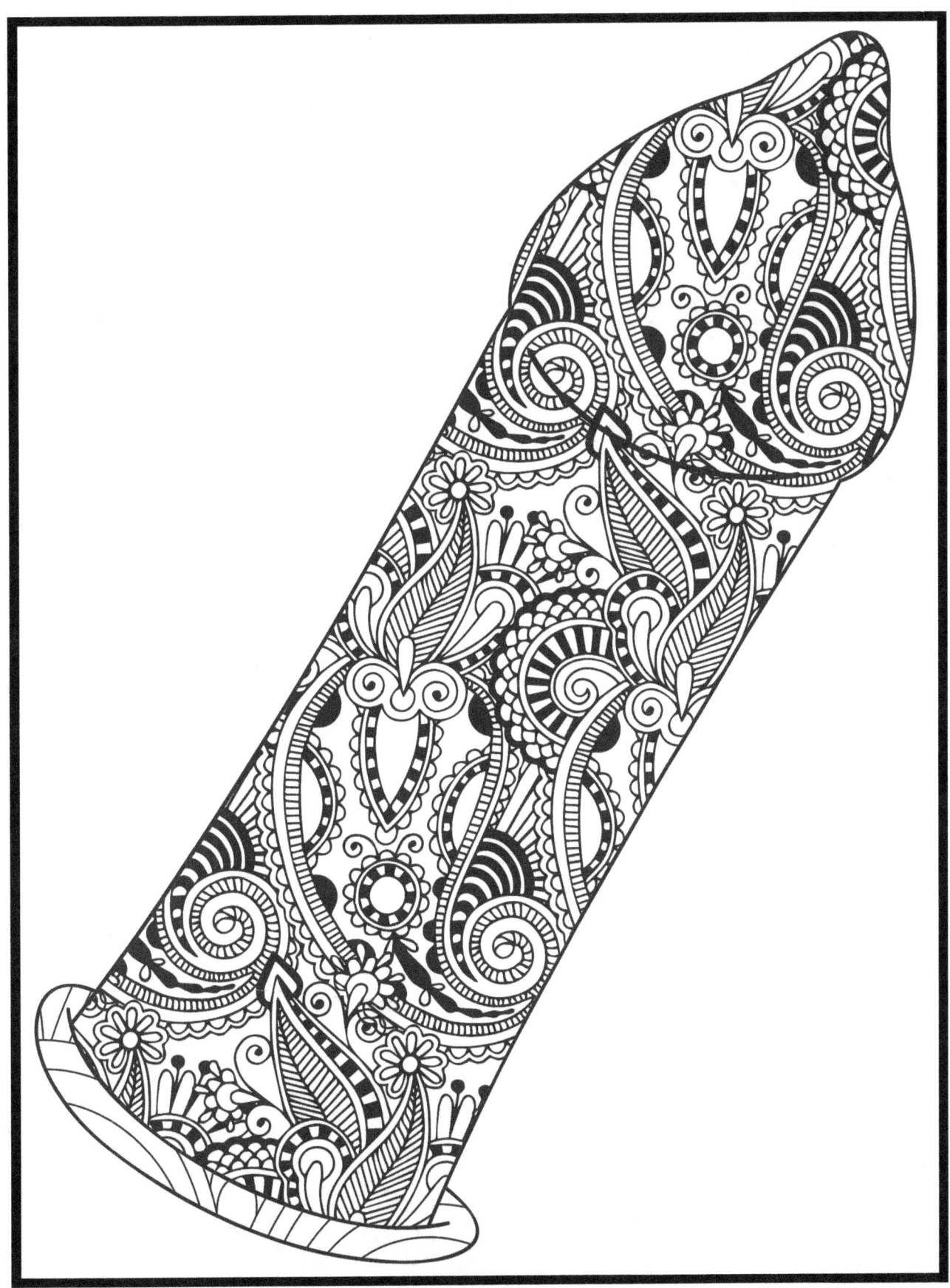

COLOR TEST PAGE

COLOR TEST PAGE

www.ingramcontent.com/pod-product-compliance
Lightning Source LLC
Chambersburg PA
CBHW081257180526
45170CB00007B/2470